Rachel Carson

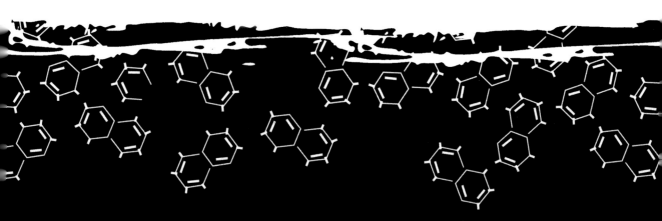

Anita Croy

CRABTREE

PUBLISHING COMPANY

WWW.CRABTREEBOOKS.COM

CRABTREE
PUBLISHING COMPANY
WWW.CRABTREEBOOKS.COM

Author: Anita Croy
Editors: Sarah Eason, Melissa Boyd, Ellen Rodger
Proofreader and indexer: Jennifer Sanderson
Proofreader: Wendy Scavuzzo
Editorial director: Kathy Middleton
Design: Paul Myerscough and Lynne Lennon
Photo research: Rachel Blount
Print coordinator: Katherine Berti

Written, developed, and produced by Calcium

Photo Credits:
t=Top, c=Center, b=Bottom, l= Left, r=Right

Inside: CDC: Public Health Image Library: p. 18; Flickr: Smithsonian Institution: p. 4; Shutterstock: Africa Studio: p. 59; Alexblacksea: p. 31b; Sk Hasan Ali: p. 56; ArtMari: p. 7tr; Michal Balada: p. 22; Jon Bilous: p. 6; Willyam Bradberry: p. 12; Catwalker: p. 20; Marusya Chaika: p. 7bl; Klanarong Chitmung: p. 34; Dreamframer: p. 32; Cecil Bo Dzwowa: p. 41b; Isabel Eve: p. 27t; Everett Historical: pp. 15, 36, 40; Fon.tepsoda: p. 27b; Nicole S Glass: p. 58; Grop: p. 30b; Shane Gross: p. 16; Herjua: p. 45; Jesus Giraldo Gutierrez: p. 51b; Jane_Mori: p. 47bl; Stephan Kerkhofs: p. 17t; Nickolay Khoroshkov: p. 21br; Tomasz Klejdysz: p. 19t; George Lamson: p. 55; Doug Lemke: p. 26; Lucky Graphic: p. 41tr; Jason Mintzer: p. 44; Muph: p. 37t; Oleksandrum: p. 31t; Andrew Opila: p. 14; Charles T. Peden: p. 28; Pisaphotography: p. 21t; PongMoji: p. 35; Olga Popova: p. 42; Lee Prince: p. 57; Marina Pushkareva: p. 11; Tom Reichner: p. 8; RetroClipArt: p. 37b; Kate Scott: p. 30c; Carolina K. Smith MD: p. 19b; Sundra: pp. 48t, 49b; Tigergallery: p. 25; Bodor Tivadar: p. 61b; Lone Wolf Photography: p. 10; U.S. Fish and Wildlife Service Museum/Archives: pp. 24, 29; Wikimedia Commons: Walter Albertin/Library of Congress: p. 54; Eli.pousson: p. 46; Internet Archive Book Images: p. 7c; LFSM: p. 38; Laura A. Macaluso, Ph.D: p. 60; NASA/Apollo 17 crew; taken by either Harrison Schmitt or Ron Evan: p. 52; Rex Gary Schmidt/U. S. Fish and Wildlife Service: p. 50; White House Press Office (WHPO): p. 39; Andreas Trepte, www.photo-natur.net: p. 17b; U.S. Fish and Wildlife Service Headquarters: p. 61t; The U.S. Food and Drug Administration: p. 51t; U. S. National Archives and Records Administration: p. 9; USPS, scanned by Greudin: p. 48b; Frank Wolfe: p. 49t; Xanthis: p. 47br.

Library and Archives Canada Cataloguing in Publication

Title: Rachel Carson / Anita Croy.
Names: Croy, Anita, author.
Description: Series statement: Scientists who changed the world | Includes index.
Identifiers: Canadiana (print) 2020022607X | Canadiana (ebook) 20200226096 | ISBN 9780778782209 (hardcover) | ISBN 9780778782261 (softcover) | ISBN 9781427126122 (HTML)
Subjects: LCSH: Carson, Rachel, 1907-1964—Juvenile literature. | LCSH: Biologists—Biography—Juvenile literature. | LCSH: Environmentalists—Biography—Juvenile literature. | LCSH: Science writers—Biography—Juvenile literature. | LCGFT: Biographies.
Classification: LCC QH31.C37 C76 2021 | DDC j570.92—dc23

Library of Congress Cataloging-in-Publication Data

Names: Croy, Anita, author.
Title: Rachel Carson / Anita Croy.
Description: New York : Crabtree Publishing Company, 2021. | Series: Scientists who changed the world | Includes index.
Identifiers: LCCN 2020017173 (print) | LCCN 2020017174 (ebook) | ISBN 9780778782209 (hardcover) | ISBN 9780778782261 (paperback) | ISBN 9781427126122 (ebook)
Subjects: LCSH: Carson, Rachel, 1907-1964--Juvenile literature. | Marine biologists--United States--Biography--Juvenile literature. | Environmentalists--United States--Biography--Juvenile literature.
Classification: LCC QH91.3.C3 C76 2021 (print) | LCC QH91.3.C3 (ebook) | DDC 508.092 [B]--dc23
LC record available at https://lccn.loc.gov/2020017173
LC ebook record available at https://lccn.loc.gov/2020017174

Crabtree Publishing Company
www.crabtreebooks.com   1-800-387-7650

Printed in the U.S.A./082020/CG20200601

Published in Canada
Crabtree Publishing
616 Welland Ave.
St. Catharines, Ontario
L2M 5V6

Published in the United States
Crabtree Publishing
347 Fifth Ave
Suite 1402-145
New York, NY 10016

Published in the United Kingdom
Crabtree Publishing
Maritime House
Basin Road North, Hove
BN41 1WR

Published in Australia
Crabtree Publishing
3 Charles Street
Coburg North
VIC, 3058

Contents

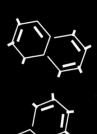

CHAPTER 1

This photograph shows Rachel Carson in around 1951.

RACHEL CARSON
Biography

Born: May 27, 1907

Place of birth: Springdale, Pennsylvania, United States

Mother: Maria McLean Carson

Father: Robert Warden Carson

Famous for: Altering the course of history by alerting the world to the dangers of **environmental** poisoning from **pesticides** and other human-made farming chemicals.

How she changed the world: Rachel Carson's writings, including her bestselling book *Silent Spring*, warned the world of the great environmental catastrophe humanity faced if it continued to alter nature through its behavior.

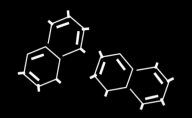

Carson said that
the twentieth century
was the only CENTURY
in history when a single
species, HUMANS,
had acquired significant
POWER to change
the NATURE of the
whole WORLD.

Rachel L. Carson

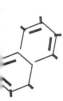

COUNTRY GIRL

Rachel Carson was born in 1907, the youngest of Maria and Robert Carson's three children. Much younger than her sister and brother, Rachel spent her childhood roaming her family's 65-acre (26-ha) lot of woods and fields, as well as the surrounding countryside in rural Pennsylvania. Inspired by her mother, who taught her how to recognize different bird songs and to identify the stars in the night sky, Rachel loved nature from an early age.

Her best friends were wild birds and creatures.

When she was just 11, a short story Rachel wrote was published in a popular children's magazine called *St. Nicholas*. Rachel made up her mind that she would be a writer. When she was not writing, she was out exploring every inch of the countryside. She was a loner who said that, apart from her mom, her best friends were wild birds and creatures.

In high school, Rachel was a straight-A student who graduated first in her class in 1923. Her mom kept her at home whenever there was an outbreak of a **contagious** disease, and she spent that time reading. Her father could not find a job that paid regularly, and the family's financial situation got worse as Rachel grew older. To make ends meet, her mom taught piano. Her mom was determined that Rachel would have every chance that her mom had missed.

Rachel grew up surrounded by farmland and woodland in Pennsylvania.

Carson said that the aim of science was to discover and reveal truth, which was also the aim of forms of writing such as biography or history—so she believed that science writing was not a separate field of its own.

Exploring the ideas

Rachel Carson wanted to be a writer from an early age. As an undergraduate at the Pennsylvania College for Women (PCW), she switched her major from English to **biology** in her second year thanks to her inspirational biology teacher, Mary Scott Skinker. In the 1920s, nobody thought students could study English and biology at the same time, as students were expected to major either in science or the arts. Carson was **trailblazing** because she loved both and realized they could be combined. Once she had switched to biology, she focused her writing on scientific subjects.

Pennsylvania College for Women was founded in Pittsburgh in 1869. Today, it is known as Chatham University.

HISTORY'S STORY

Biology teacher Mary Scott Skinker (1891–1948) was an influential **mentor** for Carson and later a great friend. Thanks to the glamorous Skinker, who knew many of the key scientists in the **marine biology** world, Carson landed an internship in summer 1929 at the U.S. Marine Laboratory at Woods Hole, Massachusetts, which helped launch her career.

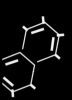

A LOVE OF NATURE

Carson had spent much of her childhood studying nature. She knew the names of all the birds and plants around her family home in Springdale. This knowledge would help her love for the natural world grow. It was also useful not just while she was a student at college, but beyond college into **graduate school**, then work.

Carson's attention to detail and willingness to study made her a model student, but her family's unstable financial situation meant she relied on **scholarships** and other financial help to attend college. When Mary Scott Skinker announced she was leaving PCW for Johns Hopkins University, Carson decided to apply there, even though she had not yet graduated from PCW. She won a place in April 1928 to study for a master's degree, or higher degree, in **zoology**. But even with scholarships she could not raise the money to attend. When she reapplied, having graduated from PCW in 1929, her plan came together.

Carson was familiar with birds such as the chipping sparrow, whose piercing call can be heard at night as it migrates south for the winter.

Summer work

While Carson studied for her master's, she spent her summer vacations working. In 1929, she spent a perfect summer at the Marine Biology Laboratory in Woods Hole, where she worked alongside other talented scientists as they studied the ocean. She tutored over the next summers, until she graduated in 1932. Not only did she need to earn money for her studies, but her family was growing more and more dependent on her.

During the Great Depression, millions of Americans lost their jobs and had to rely on **soup kitchens** to eat.

Supporting her family

Carson hoped to complete her studies in marine biology with a doctor of philosophy degree (PhD). However, the effects of the **Great Depression** were growing worse. Many people were without jobs and living in poverty. In summer 1934, Carson was forced to drop out of her PhD course because she had no money. Things grew worse for her family the next summer, when her father died suddenly at the age of 71. Carson's sister, Marian, was ill and unable to work. She and her two daughters were living in the family home, and Carson was now the only one able to earn money. Throughout her life, Carson always put her family first.

Having watched her father struggle to provide for the family, Carson knew a government job would provide the regular income the family desperately needed. In 1935, she took the Federal Civil Service exams to become a junior wildlife biologist and junior **aquatic** biologist in the U.S. Bureau of Fisheries. Skinker helped her prepare for the tough examinations, which she passed. The only problem was there were no openings.

FIRST STEPS AS A WRITER

Carson had the skills, but there was no job available. Luckily, there was soon an unusual assignment for which the department head, Elmer Higgins, needed help. Higgins remembered interviewing Carson a few months earlier and thought she might just be the right person. His decision changed the course of Carson's life.

The U.S. Bureau of Fisheries was putting together a series of 52 radio shows on sea life called *Romance Under the Waters*. The idea was to make marine biology interesting for the average listener, which was proving a challenge. Higgins asked Carson if she could write one or two scripts to see if she could improve on what the bureau was producing. He was taking a chance, because he had never read anything Carson had written.

Carson's scripts were so good that Higgins asked her to write an introduction to marine life for a government brochure. Carson began an essay she called "The World of Waters." She decided to turn some of her scripts into articles about the marine life of Chesapeake Bay. She sent them to the local newspaper, the *Baltimore Sun*, which published them.

Carson's newspaper articles about Chesapeake Bay (pictured) focused on the need to conserve and respect the sea.

"The World of Waters"

When Elmer Higgins read Carson's essay, he realized immediately that it would be wasted in a government pamphlet. He thought it was a work of literature and should be in the leading literary magazine of the day, *The Atlantic Monthly*. Carson was thrilled, and made the changes Higgins suggested before sending her work off to the magazine.

Carson's career was suddenly starting to fall into place. In July 1936, she was finally hired as a junior aquatic biologist at the U.S. Bureau of Fisheries in Washington, DC. With her government salary and her writing jobs, she was able to provide for her mom and extended family. The death of her sister in January 1937 left Carson and her mom as guardians for her two nieces. To cut down on her travel time to work, she moved the family to Silver Spring, Maryland, in June 1937. Finally, in July 1937, she heard back from *The Atlantic Monthly* about "The World of Waters." The magazine wanted to publish her essay.

Carson was fascinated by sea creatures such as the Dungeness crab, which sheds its shell to allow its body to grow.

HISTORY'S STORY

The Great Depression (1929–1939) was a period of terrible hardship that began in the United States and spread around the world. Businesses closed up and people's savings became worthless. Millions of Americans lost their jobs at a time when there was very little government support.

CHAPTER 2

Carson believed that studying sea creatures, such as dolphins, revealed the importance of the oceans to all life on Earth.

THE NATURAL WORLD
Background

In the early 1800s, scientists were developing a new approach to biology called ecology. It studies how **organisms** relate to one another and their environment. Several branches developed:

- **Behavioral ecology:** the study of how an animal's behavior evolves, or changes over time, because of its environment

- **Cognitive ecology:** the study of how animals gather information about the environment, relate it to themselves, and use it to survive

- **Social ecology:** the study of the relationships between people and their environment

- **Coevolution:** the study of how the **evolution** of two different **species** can affect each other

- **Biogeography:** the study of where animals and plants live

- **Molecular ecology:** the study of the **genes** of animals and plants and how they relate to their environment

- **Human ecology:** the study of the relationship between humans and their natural and human-made environments

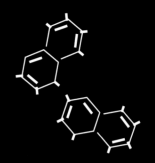

Carson said that the more people FOCUSED their attention on the WONDERS of the world around them, the less they would want to DESTROY the WORLD.

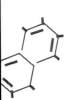
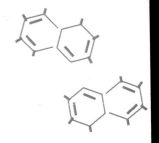

SAVING THE ENVIRONMENT

The environmental movement in America started in the late 1800s with the aim of protecting the West, as the population expanded westward. The tone had been set earlier in the century by the writer Henry David Thoreau (1817–1862). His book *Walden; or, Life in the Woods* (1854) inspired the environmental movement with its description of living a simple life in tune with nature.

...to explore, enjoy, and protect the wild places of the earth.

Building on Thoreau's ideas was the **naturalist** John Muir (1838–1914), known as "John of the Mountains," who founded the Sierra Club in 1892. Its mission statement was "to explore, enjoy, and protect the wild places of the earth." He also helped create the first National Park, Yosemite, in 1890.

Today, around 4 million people a year visit Yosemite National Park in California.

In 1905, President Theodore Roosevelt (1858–1919) created the United States Forest Service (USFS), which established 150 National Forests, protecting around 230 million acres (93 million ha) of public land. He set aside more than 150 million acres (61 million ha) for a series of national parks, and signed five parks into law. In 1916, President Woodrow Wilson (1856–1924) created the National Park Service, which now oversees more than 85 million acres (34 million ha) of the United States.

Ideas that changed the world

Carson wrote that humans stood at a place where the road forked. She said the road people had been traveling on seemed easy and offered rapid progress, but that it would lead to disaster. The other fork of the road was less traveled, but offered humanity the only way to reach a destination that would guarantee Earth was saved.

Exploring the ideas

By the 1960s, **environmentalists** such as Carson were aware of the damage caused by the rapid **industrialization** that followed **World War II** (1939–1945). From her earliest writings in the 1930s, Carson warned what would happen if humanity continued to sleepwalk into the future. In her view, companies and governments seeking to achieve rapid progress had polluted Earth so much that permanent damage was certain.

President Theodore Roosevelt visited Glacier Point in Yosemite in 1903.

HISTORY'S STORY

President Theodore Roosevelt was very proud of his achievement of creating a series of national parks. A lifelong **trophy hunter**, he had witnessed the destruction of wild species and knew that, if nothing was done to protect the natural world, the situation would get worse. **Conservation** became one of his key concerns during his presidency, which lasted from 1901 to 1909.

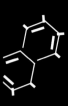

THE MARINE WORLD

Carson spent much of her career as a full-time employee at the U.S. Bureau of Fisheries, where she worked between 1936 and 1952. Marine biology remained her priority. She had studied it at college and she loved nothing more than to be by the ocean, observing its abundance of life. The ocean, she believed, had a lot to teach us.

What fascinated Carson about the ocean was that, on the surface, it looked as though nothing much was happening. As soon as you went to the edge of the water or dived deep below the surface, however, it was clear that the ocean was teeming with life. She wanted her writing to give people who were not marine biologists an idea of what was going on in the waters that covered 71 percent of Earth's surface.

Following on from "Undersea," which was what *The Atlantic Monthly* renamed "The World of Waters," Carson wanted to produce a longer book that gave as accurate an account of the ocean and the creatures that lived in it as possible. One of her interests was the ecological relationships between the different forms of ocean life that have existed for billions of years.

Carson wanted people to be excited about creatures such as the green sea turtle, as well as about how it meshed with the seagrass beds where it lived.

Under the Sea-Wind

Carson's book *Under the Sea-Wind*, which was published in 1941, was divided into three sections. One section dealt with a seabird, *Rynchops*, a black skimmer; the second section with *Scomber*, a mackerel; and the final section with pond creatures such as eels and ducks. She often wrote as though she was on the ocean floor and was seeing the ocean through the eyes of the creatures she described. She wanted the general reader to understand that the organisms that inhabit the ocean return to the seabed when they die, becoming part of an ongoing process of life, death, and decay. For her, that was the majesty and importance of the oceans.

Mackerel swim together in huge groups called shoals.

Early warnings

While she worked on her book, Carson did not neglect her marine biology duties. She wrote scientific reports and analyzed **data** about fish in the Atlantic Ocean. She published extensively for the Bureau of Fisheries, not just on fish but on other wildlife. She appeared at conferences, where she was already warning that the drop in wildlife numbers was linked to human behavior.

Black skimmers live in large, noisy groups on sandy beaches.

NEW PESTICIDES

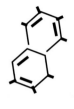

World War II was finally brought to an end in August 1945, when the United States dropped two **atomic bombs** on the Japanese cities of Hiroshima and Nagasaki. The use of these bombs brought about the atomic age—period in time that emphasized technology. Scientists worried that conservation would be left behind.

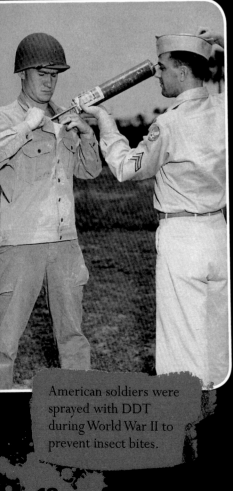

American soldiers were sprayed with DDT during World War II to prevent insect bites.

Among the rapid developments that followed the war was the appearance of a new type of pesticide. These chemicals were sprayed on crops to protect them from insects that could devastate the harvest. For some time, Carson and her colleagues had been reading the test results about a human-made pesticide named dichlorodiphenyl-trichloroethane, known more simply as DDT. The biologists in the Fish and Wildlife divisions of the Bureau of Fisheries had produced reports on the impact DDT had on fish and other wildlife.

DDT was also known to work as an insect repellent on humans, and the U.S. Army had used it during the war to protect soldiers from lice and other insects. Soon, it was being discussed as a miracle pesticide that could revolutionize farming by waging a war against insects that attack crops. For all those who were enthusiastic about this new chemical, there were those who were already cautioning against its possible harmful side effects.

Green Revolution

In the years after the war, **agriculture** was changing fast, with larger farms, bigger fields, and greater profits. This was part of a movement known as the Green Revolution, which aimed to improve farming not just in the United States but across the world. As populations grew and there were more mouths to feed, farming used more and more machines. Farmers welcomed new pesticides and human-made **fertilizers**, which helped them grow more crops. These new chemicals allowed intensive, or heavy, farming where farmers did not have to leave their fields empty after the harvest to allow the soil to recover. DDT was sprayed from small aircraft across millions of acres of U.S. farmland.

Farmers wanted to protect their crops from pests such as the European corn borer.

Using aircraft was the only efficient way to spray the large areas of crops on many U.S. farms.

HISTORY'S STORY

The Green Revolution was a set of plans that used the latest technology to allow farmers to produce crops on a much larger scale than before. It peaked during the 1950s and 1960s, when a combination of the new pesticides, fertilizers, irrigation, and machines dramatically increased crops. The Green Revolution was seen as a scientific solution to the problem of how to feed a growing global population.

ENVIRONMENTAL MILESTONES 1890–1960

1892 The Sierra Club is founded by John Muir to protect the environment.

1903 President Theodore Roosevelt creates the first National Bird Preserve.

1908 Roosevelt sets up the National Conservation Commission.

1909 Roosevelt calls the first North American Conservation Conference.

1916 The National Parks Service is created to conserve and enhance the natural and cultural heritage.

1919 The National Parks Conservation Association is founded. Its mission is to educate the American public about its National Parks.

1934 The Everglades Act is passed. It paves the way for the Everglades National Park to be created in Florida.

1934 The Fish and Wildlife Coordination Act is passed to protect fish and wildlife from federal activity in the water.

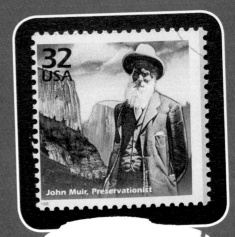

John Muir, Preservationist

This stamp celebrating John Muir was issued in 1998.

Despite the 1934 Everglades act, human activity has left the Everglade wetlands short of water.

1935 The Wilderness Society is formed with the aim of protecting America's wilderness and inspiring Americans to care for wild places.

1947 Defenders of Wildlife is founded to protect native animals and plants across the United States.

1948 The International Union for Conservation of Nature is founded. Based in Switzerland, it is dedicated to conserving natural resources.

The 1955 act was the first attempt to limit factories releasing smoke and gas.

1951 The Nature Conservancy, an environmental organization, is founded. Its aim is to preserve the land and water on which all life depends.

1955 The Air Pollution Control Act is passed, recognizing the declining air quality across America's cities.

1958 Levels of **carbon dioxide**, a harmful gas produced by pollution, are monitored in Earth's **atmosphere** for the first time.

CHAPTER 3

Carson believed that the region where the sea met the land was one of the most important **ecosystems** on Earth.

A POWERFUL CASE
Breakthrough

Carson had a long career with the U.S. Bureau of Fisheries, which was later renamed the U.S. Fish and Wildlife Service:

1935: Passes the exam for the Bureau of Fisheries

1936: Hired as a junior aquatic biologist

1939: Promoted to associate aquatic biologist

1941: Transfers to the Chicago office

1943: Promoted to aquatic biologist

1943: Moves back to the Washington, DC office

1952: Resigns from the Fish and Wildlife Service to write full time

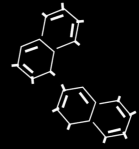

Carson said that to stand at the edge of the SEA, watching the TIDES and BIRDS that had flown above the SURF for many thousands of years, was to know things as nearly ETERNAL as any EARTHLY life could be.

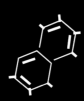

BESTSELLING BOOK

For a book that would win the 1952 National Book Award for Nonfiction and stay on the *New York Times* bestseller list for 86 weeks, *The Sea Around Us* had a difficult start. Carson struggled to find a publisher. Only when it was made into a series in the *New Yorker* magazine in 1951 did the book really grab attention.

As we destroy the land, we will become more dependent on the ocean.

The Sea Around Us was the second of what would become Carson's **trilogy** on the sea. The book takes the reader from the sea's earliest days to the latest discoveries about it. She wanted the reader to understand just how dependent humans are on the ocean. She argued that, as we destroy the land, we will become more dependent on the ocean. The book was turned down by 20 publishers before Oxford University Press finally agreed to publish it.

Carson (right) explores sea life in the warm shallows just offshore.

However, once the book was published, the shy Carson was suddenly flooded with fan mail and requests for interviews. What made the book so popular was Carson's poetic style of writing. She was a star! She even gave permission for a documentary movie to be made based on the book. When the movie came out, however, she hated it and refused to have anything to do with it.

Ideas that changed the world

Carson wrote that it was a curious situation that the sea, where life on Earth had begun, should now be threatened by one of the forms of life on Earth: humans. She said that the sea, although damaged, would continue to exist. What might not survive was life itself.

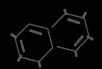

Exploring the ideas

Carson's constant study of the ocean and ocean life while she worked at the U.S. Fish and Wildlife Service made her well placed to see for herself the changes pollution from humans was making to the ocean. She understood that, since the oceans cover more than two-thirds of Earth's surface, they would have the ability to adapt and change. If humans continued on their path of self-interest and destroyed more of the environment, it would ultimately be humanity that would pay the price, not the oceans.

Oil washed ashore from a leaking pipe is cleared off a beach in Thailand in 2013.

HISTORY'S STORY

Throughout her life, Carson had female mentors and close friendships. They started with her mother and Mary Scott Skinker. In 1953, when Carson was already famous, she met Dorothy Freeman and her husband, Stanley. The two women shared a love of nature. They remained best friends until Carson's death, writing to each other often when they were apart.

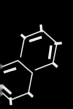

THE EDGE OF THE SEA

The success of *The Sea Around Us* allowed Carson to quit her day job to concentrate on writing full time. Its success also led to the reissue of her first book, *Under the Sea-Wind*. It quickly became a bestseller, too. In 1955, Carson published the final book in her three sea books, *The Edge of the Sea*.

Carson's new-found fame allowed her to write the book she had always wanted to write about the ocean. *The Edge of the Sea* was an account of the ecology of the Atlantic seashore in three different places along the East Coast: New England's rocky coastline, the sandy coastline of the Carolinas, and the coral coast of the Florida Keys.

Carson was determined that the book be not only scientifically accurate, but also be a poetic **homage** to the ocean. She included **classification** data, like in a science book. Although the book was loosely described as a "field guide," Carson knew that readers who expected a field guide would be disappointed. A field guide helps readers to identify plants and animals in the wild. Carson's book was in a much more narrative, or storytelling, style than an A–Z account.

The New England coast includes spectacular natural regions such as Arcadia National Park.

Writing like a poet

Carson explained that, to understand the ocean, it was necessary to take the time to really observe the shoreline and the way the waves roll in and out, creating a battlefield for survival for marine life. To convey this struggle, Carson chose to concentrate on detail rather than the ocean as a whole. For example, she took readers to the surf zone, where rock-clinging barnacles and periwinkles survive.

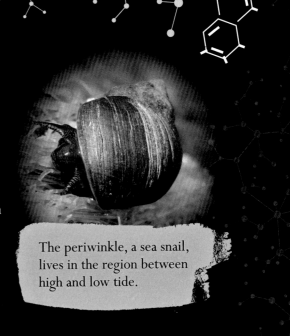

The periwinkle, a sea snail, lives in the region between high and low tide.

With *The Edge of the Sea*, Carson **pioneered** a new type of scientific literature. It was a narrative account of the biological principles that control life on the seashore and the animals that live there. She wanted to show her readers how those animals have adapted to the conditions of the seashore and why they live where they do. Carson emphasized the millions of years of evolution it had taken to get to that point. She also noted the **fragility** of that position, which humanity could so easily destroy.

Another success

Carson was trying to pull off a very tricky balance in *The Edge of the Sea*. However, after the first **installment** of the new book appeared in *The New Yorker* magazine in August 1955, it was clear to Carson's fans that she had created another bestseller.

Barnacles anchor themselves to rocks and use feeding tubes to gather food when they are underwater.

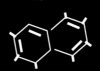

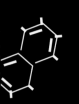

TURNING TO THE LAND

After Carson had finished the final book in her ocean trilogy, she turned her attention to the land. She wanted to study the damage being inflicted on nature by the new human-made pesticides, particularly DDT. When she was still at the Fish and Wildlife Service, Carson had started to read disturbing reports about the damage being done to marine life by DDT and other chemicals.

Before she even began to write down her ideas, Carson spent six years documenting the evidence that agricultural chemicals were being misused without their impact being fully understood. From 1957, Carson began to pay attention to federal proposals for widespread pesticide spraying, part of a program to industrialize farming.

Increasingly, Carson became convinced that this widespread use of pesticides would have a harmful effect on the environment. She realized that pesticides intended to wipe out the insect population should more accurately be called "biocides," or chemicals that poison all living things. She saw that their effects are passed to the birds that eat the insects, killing them in turn. Without birds, wildlife and plants all suffer as the whole ecosystem is damaged.

Carson was gathering evidence that birds such as the American goldfinch were under threat.

The human cost

Carson also looked at the effects pesticides had on humans. She linked their use to a rise in cases of cancer and other illnesses. Today, that link is well known, but when Carson was working, no one had publicly considered this very shocking idea. She knew she might be accused of **scaremongering**.

Like all good scientists, Carson checked her facts and listened carefully to other experts.

Checking her facts

Before Carson's book was printed, she sent it to a lot of scientific experts for their comments. She wanted to make sure she could defend all her evidence in court if necessary, as she suspected that the chemical industry would not be happy with her work. Most of the experts wrote back saying they could find no errors. Some, including the ecologist Frank Egler, went further. They wanted to help Carson by pointing out information she had left out. Carson was thrilled at Egler's careful reading of her manuscript. Another expert, Clarence Cottam, praised the quality of Carson's writing and her knowledge. He also warned that she would face ridicule and condemnation, or strong disapproval, by those who made money from pesticides.

In 1962, Carson was finally ready to publish what would become her most famous book, *Silent Spring*. It was also to become one of the key books of the environmental movement in the 1900s.

CARSON'S KEY WORKS

Under the Sea-Wind (1941)
This was the first of Carson's trilogy about the ocean, describing life beneath the waves.

The Sea Around Us (1951)
The second in her ocean trilogy, this book was a study of the processes that formed Earth, the moon, and the oceans.

The Edge of the Sea (1955)
The final part of Carson's trilogy, this was a poetic guide to identifying the creatures found in marshes, tidal areas, and shallows that border the ocean.

Tidal marshes are home to birds such as these greater yellowlegs, as well as fish, crabs, and plants.

Silent Spring (1962)

This bestseller was a thoroughly researched study of what happens to the natural world when artificial chemicals are used on it.

The Sense of Wonder (1965)

Originally a magazine article, this work was published as a book after Carson's death. It describes her philosophy that adults must **nurture** children's sense of wonder in the natural world and try to keep it as they grow older.

Pests such as Colorado potato beetles can devastate crops. The beetles eat potato leaves, killing the plants.

Lost Woods: The Discovered Writing of Rachel Carson (1998)

This collection, published after her death, included Carson's letters, speeches, and childhood prose spanning 45 years.

CHAPTER 4

Areas of North America such as California are intensively farmed, and farmers often use human-made fertilizers and **insecticides**.

SILENT SPRING
Spreading Ideas

These were Carson's key concerns in *Silent Spring*:

- The negative impact humans have on the environment

- The speed with which the natural world is being destroyed by humans

- The careless use of pesticides and their effects

- The incorrect information the chemical industry spreads about their products

- The federal government's support for the chemical industry

- The lack of scientific information about the long-term effects of pesticides, despite the fact they were in widespread use

Carson said that contemplating the BEAUTY of EARTH gives people reserves of STRENGTH throughout their whole LIVES.

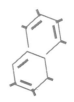

A WORLD WITHOUT BIRDS

The title of Carson's groundbreaking book *Silent Spring* referred to a world in which there would be no birdsong because the birds were dead, poisoned by the chemicals used to kill the insects they ate. Birdsong, Carson argued, is the backdrop to nature and to our daily lives.

...the history of life on Earth has been a history of interaction between living things and their surroundings.

Carson's inspiration for the book came from a friend who had noticed there were fewer birds singing after the neighboring property was sprayed with chemicals. The balance of nature had been destroyed by the pesticides. Carson observed in her book that the history of life on Earth has been a history of interaction between living things and their surroundings. Disturb that interaction, she warned, and the delicate balance of life will soon collapse.

Fire ants live on fruit trees, biting workers who try to pick the fruit.

Carson wanted people to take note of the effects that pesticides were having on the countryside. She knew enough from her research to understand that the long-term consequences of using pesticides would be much wider than just killing fire ants or other insects.

Ideas that changed the world

Carson asked why anyone would put up with a diet of weak poisons, a group of acquaintances who are not quite enemies, or the noise of motors that did not quite drive people insane. She wondered who would want to live in a world that is just not quite fatal.

Exploring the ideas

One of the revolutionary things about *Silent Spring* was Carson's call to action. She wanted ordinary people to stop accepting things done in their name by governments and industry. She saw inaction as leading people to have a **compromised** and **mediocre** life. She called on people to take responsibility, not just for themselves, but for the environment in which they lived. By so doing, she argued, people could achieve real change. Her words sparked the widespread environmental movement of the following decade.

DDT remains legal in some parts of the world. These workers are spraying DDT to kill mosquitoes in Thailand.

HISTORY'S STORY

DDT is a colorless, odorless, and tasteless chemical that was first used as an insecticide during World War II. After the war, it was used in agriculture to kill insects. From the beginning, some scientists believed that DDT was harmful, but the chemical industry and government played down its side-effects. It was not banned for agricultural use in the United States until 1972.

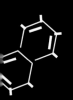

FURIOUS BACKLASH

When *Silent Spring* was published in 1962, Carson was a popular and well-respected writer. She knew that her findings would cause **controversy**, but she was not prepared for just how nasty the **backlash** from the chemical industry would be. It started even before the book was on the shelves, as word of its contents spread. Much of the attack was directed at Carson herself rather than what she had written.

Carson thought the pesticide crisis was just as severe as the...fear of a nuclear attack.

Carson had deliberately used a powerful tone to persuade her readers of the urgent need for change. Carson held the government and the scientific establishment responsible for allowing human-made pesticides to be sold widely. She asked them to reconsider their position, although she did not ask for an outright ban of DDT. She thought the pesticide crisis was just as severe as the great threat that dominated the decade, which was the fear of a nuclear attack. *Silent Spring* was published on September 27, 1962, just before the Cuban Missile Crisis. For a brief time in October, it looked as though Soviet nuclear weapons would be launched against the United States from Cuba.

During the Cuban Missile Crisis, a U.S. Navy ship and airplane head off a Soviet cargo vessel heading for Cuba.

Huge chemical factories have been built to make fertilizers and pesticides for intensive agriculture.

Angry business

Not even Carson's harshest critic could have expected the size of the campaign waged against her by chemical companies who were afraid that she would cause a drop in sales. She was accused of being stupid, arrogant, and irresponsible. The National Agricultural Chemicals Association (NACA) spent more than $250,000 trying to persuade the public that Carson was wrong. They did everything to discredit Carson's scientific qualifications, calling her an emotional female **alarmist**. The NACA and the Manufacturing Chemists' Association sent out brochures criticizing Carson.

One of Carson's most well-known critics was Dr. Cynthia Westcott, known as "The Plant Doctor." Wescott's popular plant column was published in many women's magazines. She tried very hard to stress her better academic qualifications over Carson's and suggested that Carson had exaggerated the threat from DDT—but she did agree that more research into insecticides was needed.

37

A LONG DEBATE

The debate over *Silent Spring* and the threat of pesticides refused to go away. It continued through 1962 and much of the following year. It remained a topic of bitter debate, on television and in the U.S. Congress.

On April 3, 1963, CBS television network aired a special show dedicated to the *Silent Spring* controversy. Between 10 and 15 million Americans watched the show. Carson read passages from her book that explained the problem, and experts from both sides gave their opinions. Before the program aired, there had been a big build-up, with many newspaper columns written about it and with fierce **lobbying** by the chemical industry.

To make sure the program was fair, its producer, Jay McMullen, had spent eight months interviewing experts and government officials who had a wide range of views about the dangers of pesticides. Following the program, however, it was clear that Carson had won the argument. Her cool and calm manner contrasted sharply with her opponents. The public was on her side. CBS received hundreds of letters praising the show. Thousands of people wrote angry letters to various government departments protesting about their policies.

RACHEL CARSON

The effects of Carson's work were felt around the world. This statue in her honor was erected in Argentina.

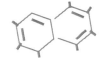
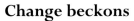

Change beckons

On May 15, 1963, President John F. Kennedy's Science Advisory Committee released its long-overdue report into pesticides. While it was not as critical of the chemical industry as many in the industry had feared, it clearly agreed with Carson and her book. It said that *Silent Spring* had brought the public's attention to the **toxicity** of pesticides.

Following the report, CBS aired a second program on the pesticide issue, concluding that Carson had two aims in writing her book: one was to alert the public and the second was to get the government to act. She had achieved both.

Carson was asked to appear in front of the President's Science Advisory Committee (PSAC). She spoke for 40 minutes and explained how pesticide pollution spread, killing far more than its intended victims. It was one of her last public appearances. By that time, Carson knew she was dying from breast cancer.

President Kennedy was an eager defender of America's coastal areas, so he knew about Carson before she wrote *Silent Spring*.

HISTORY'S STORY

The 1963 PSAC's conclusions largely supported Carson's book. As a result of the report and Carson's testimony to a U.S. Senate Subcommittee, the Senate proposed introducing two bills, or new laws. The bills would stop federal spraying without state knowledge and would require stronger warnings on pesticides about the danger to wildlife.

THE CAMPAIGN AGAINST DDT

1874 DDT is made for the first time.

1939 DDT is used as an insecticide against mosquitoes that carry the deadly disease malaria. It is the first modern human-made insecticide.

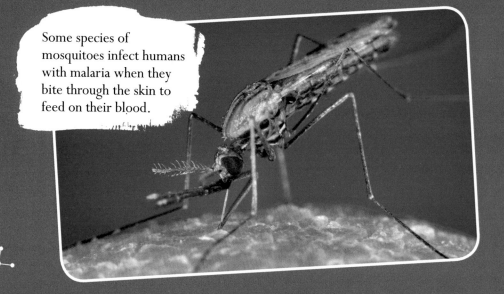

Some species of mosquitoes infect humans with malaria when they bite through the skin to feed on their blood.

1944 *Reader's Digest* magazine turns down Carson's article on DDT, saying it is too unpleasant.

1948 Paul Hermann Müller wins the Nobel Prize for Medicine for discovering the insect-killing properties of DDT.

1950 Tests show that DDT disturbs the hormones of roosters, suggesting that the chemical has potentially dangerous side effects.

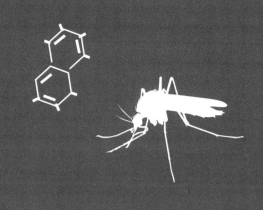

1957 The U.S. Department of Agriculture sprays pesticides across a million acres in the South to kill fire ants. The spraying kills thousands of birds. The event inspires Carson to write *Silent Spring*.

1962, August
President John F. Kennedy mentions that *Silent Spring* will soon be published and establishes a commission to look into pesticides' impact on people's health.

1962, October
Silent Spring is published. Carson does not call for the banning of pesticides, but for more controls on the use of chemicals.

1968 DDT is proven to cause cancer.

1972 The use of DDT in agriculture is banned in the United States. It is still manufactured for export to other countries.

2006 The World Health Organization (WHO) permits the indoor use of DDT in Africa to prevent the spread of malaria, which kills 445,000 to 731,000 people every year, many of them children.

The fight against malaria goes on. This boy in Zimbabwe, in southern Africa, holds a mosquito net donated by an international charity.

CHAPTER 5

Rachel Carson

This stamp celebrating Carson was released in 1981.

A TOWERING FIGURE
Reputation

Carson received many awards and honors during her lifetime, including:

- First prize for a story published in *St. Nicholas* magazine, at age 11

- The National Book Award for Non-Fiction

- The John Burroughs Medal for Nature Writing

- The Henry Grier Bryant Gold Medal of the Geographical Society

- The New York Zoological Society Gold Medal

- Election to the American Academy of Arts and Letters

- A Simon Guggenheim Fellowship

- Audubon Medal of the Audubon Society

Carson said that the HUMAN RACE was CHALLENGED more than ever before to demonstrate its MASTERY, not over NATURE, but over ITSELF.

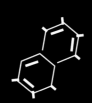

THE FIGUREHEAD

The attention *Silent Spring* received meant that Carson had become a spokeswoman for environmentalism. Her message to anyone who would listen—from President Kennedy to ordinary Americans watching TV—was that time was running out to save the planet. A lifetime of observing nature up close, and a long career in the Fish and Wildlife Service, meant that Carson was ideally placed to advise the government about what to do.

People…thanked Carson for making them sit up and pay attention.

Carson was very grateful that people had listened to her. After the publication of *Silent Spring*, more evidence was gathered showing the dangers of human-made chemicals. For example, in the early 1960s, the insecticide endrin poisoned millions of fish in the Mississippi River. Around the same time, there was a horrible scandal about the drug thalidomide, which was taken by pregnant women to help with morning sickness. The drug led to babies being born with birth defects.

People were starting to question the role of the chemicals that seemed to be everywhere in daily life, and they thanked Carson for making them sit up and pay attention. While she was writing *Silent Spring*, Carson often worried whether people would listen to her warnings. But they did.

Fish are poisoned when insecticide is washed off fields by rain and carried into rivers.

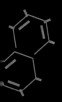

Ideas that changed the world

Carson said that if facts are the seeds that later produce knowledge and wisdom, then the emotions and the impressions of the senses are the fertile soil in which the seeds must grow.

Exploring the ideas

For Carson, it was important that people knew the facts behind the pesticides that were being used so widely. She knew that the chemical industry deliberately tried to brush over information it did not want the general public to know. Carson believed that armed with the facts, people could make up their own minds. But facts themselves are not enough. Carson believed people are made human by their emotions and the way they respond to nature. She thought if people knew that the natural world was being destroyed by pesticides, they would want to prevent it.

Carson believed that children should be encouraged to love nature, which would make them want to take care of it.

HISTORY'S STORY

People were attracted to Carson's message because she wrote so that anyone could understand the information she possessed. She also urged people to believe that they could change things. In that way, she helped to inspire a whole range of **social activism** in the 1960s that resulted in the forming of the modern environmental movement.

NOT THE END

By early 1964, Carson was weakened by her breast cancer and the intensive treatments she was being given for it. When she became sick with an infection, her condition worsened. On April 14, she died at her home in Silver Spring. Carson did not live to see DDT banned, but she had sown the seed.

The house where Carson lived in Silver Spring is now a National Historic Landmark.

Carson had not been the first or only person to speak out about DDT. By the late 1950s, it was clear to many people that there was something wrong. People living next to areas where widespread DDT spraying took place noticed that many songbirds died. As evidence based on observation started to mount, disagreements broke out with those who defended the use of DDT.

Many people in positions of power and influence helped Carson get her message about DDT across. One was Associate Justice William O. Douglas, a member of the U.S. Supreme Court and a longtime environmentalist. Douglas gave Carson some information for her chapter on **herbicides** in *Silent Spring*. Douglas had argued against his colleagues on the Supreme Court when they rejected an attempt by a group of residents in Long Island to stop the Department of Agriculture from spraying DDT in 1957. Douglas agreed with the residents that the chemical caused harm to the environment, but his colleagues on the court backed the government.

Banning DDT

Silent Spring was at the front of a powerful movement to ban the use of DDT in the United States. In 1967, the Environmental Defense Fund was formed to campaign against DDT. It succeeded in bringing lawsuits against the government on the grounds that every citizen had the right to a clean environment. Eventually the movement, along with other activist groups, succeeded. In 1972, the U.S. Environmental Protection Agency (EPA) restricted the use of DDT in agriculture to emergencies only. However, DDT is still used today to try to control malaria in parts of Africa, Asia, and South America. In India and North Korea, DDT is still sprayed onto crops as a pesticide.

Starting to question

Before *Silent Spring*, many people simply accepted the information fed to them by large corporations and governments. Despite the fact that DDT had not been properly tested, for example, an advertising campaign for the pesticide concentrated on the joys of having a bug-free home without any mention of the possible health consequences. After *Silent Spring*, the public would never be so willing to accept such claims again. Citizens were now willing to question and challenge authority.

insect spray

CONTAINING 50% DDT
RE: PATENT NO. 22,922

destroys many common insects

USE ON
POTATOES,
PEAS, CORN,
FRUITS and
ORNAMENTALS

No. 1365

NET CONTENTS 1 LB.

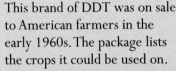

This brand of DDT was on sale to American farmers in the early 1960s. The package lists the crops it could be used on.

TURNING THE TIDE

By drawing attention to the threats to our environment, Carson kickstarted the environmental movement of the years that followed. By encouraging people to question authority and the government, she also assisted other social movements.

...humans mess with nature at their peril.

Among the movements that Carson helped to inspire was the Deep Ecology Movement. It grew up in the early 1970s on the back of the work of early environmentalists such as Carson and David Brower, who in 1969 co-founded the global environmental organization Friends of the Earth. The movement accepted Carson's description of the **interdependence** between humans and the natural world, and the fragility of the balance. The Deep Ecology Movement encouraged study of the world's **biodiversity** and ecosystems. It argued that humans mess with nature at their peril.

This set of stamps was released in 1970. They show how saving the environment had become a major concern for many Americans.

Anti-nuclear movement

The anti-nuclear movement was just beginning to take off during the 1960s. Following World War II, people had become more aware of the potential of nuclear power and its threat. For some, nuclear energy was going to save the planet by offering a "clean" source of power, but for others it was a time-bomb that had the potential to destroy Earth.

Meanwhile, the United States and the Soviet Union continued to develop new nuclear weapons as part of the long period of global tension known as the **Cold War**. Carson had warned of the threat nuclear testing posed and linked it directly to contamination that damaged animals and the environment. In 1971, Greenpeace was formed to oppose nuclear testing. Today, the organization continues its global activism.

The spirit of protest was most visible in large demonstrations against the war in Vietnam.

Protesting the Vietnam War

By highlighting the need to hold governments responsible, Carson can be seen as indirectly inspiring people to protest about many causes. One of the biggest anti-government protest movements of the 1960s and early 1970s was against the **Vietnam War** (1955–1975). Young Americans, in particular, protested a conflict they believed was unnecessary and unlawful. There were many protests and marches against the war across the United States.

49

TWENTIETH-CENTURY BIOLOGISTS AND ENVIRONMENTALISTS

Carson was one of a number of people who played a major role in making the public more aware of the threats facing the natural world.

Bob Hines (left, with Carson) was a skilled wildlife artist. He specialized in painting birds.

David Brower (1912–2000)

A world-class mountaineer, David Brower was a committed environmentalist who ran the Sierra Club from 1952 to 1969, helping it become the leading environmental membership organization in America. In 1969, he quit to help found Friends of the Earth. At the Sierra Club, he worked to preserve America's wilderness. At Friends of the Earth, he campaigned against nuclear power and the **defoliant** Agent Orange, which was used in the Vietnam War.

Bob Hines (1912–1994)

A wildlife artist at the Fish and Wildlife Service, Hines had no formal training in art or wildlife. Carson was his boss and the two worked closely together for many years, becoming good friends. She asked him to illustrate *The Edge of the Sea*. They traveled together from Maine to Florida to work on the book. After Carson found a specimen, Hines drew it, then they returned it to the wild. The book reflects their close collaboration.

Frances Oldham Kelsey (1914–2015)

Kelsey was a physician and expert in medications. In 1960, during her first month working at the U.S. Food and Drug Administration, she warned of the dangers of the drug thalidomide. Although the drug was already on sale in Germany and Great Britain, Kelsey refused to license it in the United States because she said it had not been sufficiently tested. Later, thalidomide was discovered to have caused serious birth defects in thousands of babies.

Harold L. Ickes (1874–1952)

Between 1933 and 1946, Ickes served as Secretary of the Interior in the government of President Franklin D. Roosevelt. He was responsible for the government's wide-ranging environmental program. He also worked with conservationists such as Rosalie Edge to preserve the goshawks at Hawk Mountain, Pennsylvania, which Carson visited in 1945.

Roland Clement (1912–2015)

Clement was an environmentalist who worked for two decades with the National Audubon Society, which protects birds and their habitats. He worked to preserve endangered species and set up bird sanctuaries. He was instrumental in getting DDT banned and was a very public supporter of Carson and *Silent Spring*.

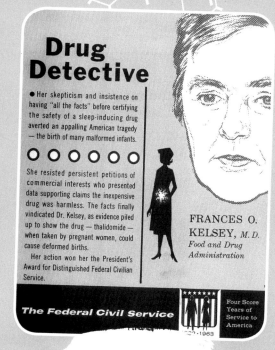

Drug Detective

● Her skepticism and insistence on having "all the facts" before certifying the safety of a sleep-inducing drug averted an appalling American tragedy — the birth of many malformed infants.

She resisted persistent petitions of commercial interests who presented data supporting claims the inexpensive drug was harmless. The facts finally vindicated Dr. Kelsey, as evidence piled up to show the drug — thalidomide — when taken by pregnant women, could cause deformed births.

Her action won her the President's Award for Distinguished Federal Civilian Service.

FRANCES O. KELSEY, M.D.
Food and Drug Administration

The Federal Civil Service

Four Score Years of Service to America

This leaflet celebrates the work of Frances Oldham Kelsey.

The goshawk is a bird of prey that hunts smaller birds and small mammals.

51

The first views of Earth from space were a dramatic warning of how fragile the planet looked from far away.

PROTECTING EARTH
Legacy

Since Carson's death, many laws have been passed to protect the environment in the United States:

1970: The Clean Air Act, which controls air pollution

1972: The Clean Water Act, which controls pollution in the nation's waters

1980: The Comprehensive Environmental Response, Compensation and Liability Act, which provides money to clean up sites damaged by pollutants such as chemicals

1982: The Nuclear Waste Policy Act, which established a national program for disposing of nuclear waste

1988: The Ocean Dumping Act, which forbids the dumping of human and industrial waste at sea

1990: The Oil Pollution Act, which makes oil companies pay for cleaning up after an oil spill

Carson said that the science of CHEMISTRY had armed itself with the most TERRIBLE WEAPONS, and that in turning those weapons against INSECTS it had also turned them against EARTH itself.

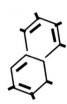

TAKING STEPS

The first humans had landed on the Moon in 1969. The photographs of Earth taken by the astronauts meant that, for the first time, people were able to see our planet from space. Its beauty was clear to see—but the images also heightened people's awareness of just how fragile Earth's resources were.

In this 1953 photo, smog caused by pollution blankets New York City.

…air and water pollution were worsening problems…

The Environmental Protection Agency (EPA) was formed in 1970 as a direct result of Carson's work in *Silent Spring*. Carson's description of the damage done by the overuse of pesticides started an outcry among the public. By the late 1960s, air and water pollution were worsening problems in many American cities. There were also a number of environmental scandals, including oil being washed up on California beaches and chemicals being spilled into the Cuyahoga River in Ohio. The government decided to act.

In 1970, President Richard Nixon outlined 37 recommendations to protect the environment, from taxing lead pollutants in gasoline to legally obliging the federal government to sort out environmental disasters. It was decided that the best way to protect America's natural resources was to set up the EPA.

Ideas that changed the world

Carson said that one way people could open their eyes was by asking themselves, "What if I had never seen this before? What if I knew I would never see it again?"

Exploring the ideas

Carson's argument in *Silent Spring* was that it had taken billions of years to create the planet we live on. In a short space of time, humans had changed the environment so rapidly that already the fragile ecosystem that had taken billions of years to evolve was under threat. She wanted to issue a stark warning. Without an immediate and dramatic change in human behavior, life on Earth could be changed beyond recognition, with species driven to extinction within a generation.

The California condor became extinct in the wild in 1987. It was successfully bred in captivity and in the wild, but remains rare.

HISTORY'S STORY

As a woman scientist, Carson was a **pioneer**. When she came up against the forces of the chemical industry, however, Carson found both her gender and her qualifications called into question, as when she was accused of being neurotic, or mentally unbalanced. Her calm handling of this treatment turned her into an icon for women in science.

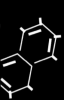

GLOBAL WARMING

As early as 1950, Carson was warning about the dangers of global warming. In *The Sea Around Us*, she described what is now widely known to be true: that the oceans hold the key to the planet's warming. At the time, scientists knew less about the role of the oceans in keeping the global climate at a steady temperature.

In *The Sea Around Us*, Carson explained the theories of the Swedish oceanographer Otto Pettersson (1848–1941), whose investigations into the deep ocean revealed a lot about how the ocean affects climate. Pettersson described huge underwater waves at the bottom of the ocean, which he called "moon waves." He suggested that these waves affected weather patterns. Depending on the intensity of the waves, the climate alternated between periods of extreme cold, known as ice ages, and more moderate temperatures. Pettersson described how glaciers would melt and sea waters would rise if the climate was too warm. He explained that a tiny increase of 1 or 2 inches (2.5–5 cm) would be enough to permanently submerge tropical islands such as the Maldives in the Indian Ocean.

Dhaka, in Bangladesh, often floods. The whole low-lying country is under threat from rising sea levels.

Melting glaciers drop walls of ice into the oceans. This process is known as calving.

Rising sea levels

Today, scientists know that the warnings of Carson, Pettersson, and others were correct. Global warming has sped up due to carbon dioxide being released into the atmosphere from burning **fossil fuels**. Rising temperatures have led glaciers to melt and sea levels to rise. The balance of the oceans and land is so sensitive that even a tiny further temperature increase might cause disaster. Some countries live with the constant threat of flooding. Bangladesh, in Asia, for example, lies barely 33 feet (10 m) above sea level. In 2019, the United Nations (UN) announced that sea levels are rising faster than ever and that immediate action is needed to avert disaster in many countries.

Warming planet

The four years before 2019 were the warmest years on record. Levels of carbon dioxide in the atmosphere are at record highs. Most scientists agree that pollution caused by human activities is to blame for increasingly extreme weather events, such as storms, floods, droughts, and forest fires. Sea levels rose by 0.15 inches (3.7 mm) in 2018, which was higher than the average of the previous 30 years.

Such evidence clearly shows that global warming is speeding up, just as Carson warned in the 1950s. Her knowledge of the fragile ecosystems that make up the oceans meant that she noticed changes before they had really made any kind of impact. She also knew that what happens in the oceans today happens to the rest of the planet tomorrow. Today, most people agree that doing something about climate change and global warming is becoming a pressing issue.

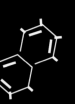

UNFINISHED CAMPAIGN

Not everyone agrees with the warnings that Carson and later environmentalists gave the world about climate change. There are still a significant number of people who claim that there has been no overall change to the climate. They deny that global warming exists, and say that Earth's temperature has always risen and fallen.

One of the people who denies global warming is Donald Trump, who was elected U.S. president at the end of 2016. Trump disagreed with experts who said the climate is changing, and argued that climate change is a hoax to damage American industry. He said that it was not fair to expect the United States to cut carbon dioxide emissions if **economic** powers such as China did not do the same. The Chinese argued that they were simply trying to modernize and that once they had caught up with the Western world, they would be able to better address their pollution problem.

THE CLIMATE IS CHANGING WHY AREN'T WE?

Modern-day environmentalists ask many of the same questions Carson first raised in the 1950s.

Taking responsibility

While politicians argue about who should take responsibility, experts agree that time is running out to stop damaging Earth in ways that cannot be reversed. Carbon dioxide and the other **greenhouse gases** that cause climate change are now at the highest levels they have been for 800,000 years. Greenhouse gases are released by many modern-day activities, such as driving cars, using air-conditioning, and burning fossil fuels such as coal.

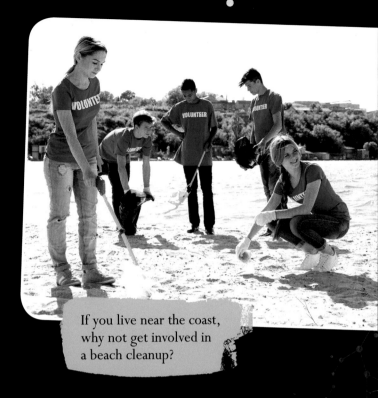

If you live near the coast, why not get involved in a beach cleanup?

In 2016, the Paris Agreement came into force. It was a unique agreement to battle climate change among 55 leading nations that account for at least 55 percent of global carbon dioxide emissions, including the United States. By early 2017, the number of countries who had signed the agreement had risen to 125. In June 2017, President Trump announced that the United States would withdraw from the agreement, starting in 2020.

What can one person do?

It is easy to make small changes, from recycling your soda can to choosing to walk or cycle to school instead of getting a ride. People are widely coming to look at Earth as a precious resource that needs to be nurtured. Its resources will not last forever, and humankind has to learn to conserve what we have. Once all the fish have been fished from the sea, there will be none left for future generations. By moderating our behavior now, as Carson suggested, we can ensure that future generations can enjoy our beautiful planet as much as we have.

LATER HONORS FOR CARSON

Since her death, Carson's reputation has grown and her influence has been widely recognized in a remarkable series of honors, including:

1973: Carson is inducted into the National Women's Hall of Fame in Seneca Falls, New York.

1975: Rachel Carson Trail, a hiking trail near Pittsburgh, is named in her honor.

1980: The Presidential Medal of Freedom is awarded by President Jimmy Carter. This is the highest award that can be given to an American civilian.

1991: Rachel Carson House, the home where Carson wrote *Silent Spring*, becomes a National Historic Landmark.

1991: The Rachel Carson Prize is founded in Stavanger, Norway. It is awarded to women who have made outstanding progress in protecting the environment.

This statue of Carson was erected at Woods Hole in Massachusetts, home of the U.S. Marine Biology Laboratory, where she once worked.

The Rachel Carson National Wildlife Refuge in Maine protects salt marshes, beaches, and estuaries.

2004: The Rachel Carson Award is founded. It is given every year by the Audubon Society to an American woman who has advanced conservation both nationally and globally.

2006: Rachel Carson Bridge in Pittsburgh, Pennsylvania, is named in her honor.

2016: Rachel Carson College is named in her honor at the University of California at Santa Cruz.

GLOSSARY

agriculture The science or practice of farming

alarmist Someone who exaggerates a danger and causes needless panic

aquatic Of or relating to water

atmosphere The blanket of gases that surrounds Earth

atomic bombs Powerful bombs that release energy from the nuclei of atoms

biodiversity The variety of plant and animal life

biology The branch of science that studies living things

carbon dioxide A colorless, odorless gas that is naturally present in the air but is also produced by burning fossil fuels

classification The arrangement of animals and plants in groups, such as species

Cold War The period of tension between the United States and Soviet Union, lasting from 1945 to 1990

compromised Accepted low standards

conservation Protection from waste or harm, particularly of plants and animals

contagious Passed from one person to another

controversy A long, public disagreement

data Information collected for study

defoliant A chemical that removes leaves from plants

economic Relating to the money, industry, and trade of a country

ecosystems All the living things in certain areas and the ways that they affect each other

environmental Relating to the natural world, or the surroundings in which a plant or animal lives

environmentalists People who are concerned about protecting the environment

evolution The process by which life has developed from earlier life forms

fertilizers Substances added to the soil to make crops grow better

fossil fuels Coal, oil, and natural gas, formed over millions of years from the remains of living things

fragility State of being easily broken or damaged

genes Instructions for appearance and behavior that are found in the cells of living things

graduate school A university school that offers programs beyond a bachelor's degree

Great Depression A severe economic downturn, starting in 1929 and lasting through the 1930s

greenhouse gases Gases that absorb the Sun's heat, trapping it in Earth's atmosphere

herbicides Chemicals that kill weeds

homage An expression of great respect

industrialization An increase in the number of factories and the use of machinery

insecticides Chemicals that kill insects

installment One of several parts of something that appears at intervals

interdependence Unable to exist without each other

internship The position of a student or trainee to work, sometimes without pay, to gain work experience

lobbying Trying to influence people in power

marine biology The branch of biology that studies the ocean

mediocre Not very good

mentor An experienced and trusted advisor

naturalist A person who studies animals and plants

nurture To care for something as it grows

organisms Living things, from bacteria to animals

pesticides Chemicals used to kill insects or other living things that destroy crops

pioneer Someone who is the first to develop a new area of knowledge

pioneered Led the way

scaremongering Spreading frightening stories

scholarships Grants or payments made to support a student's education and based on academic or other type of achievement

social activism Trying to bring about change in how people or governments behave

soup kitchens A place, especially during the Great Depression, where free food is served to homeless or very poor people

species A group of living things that look similar and can breed with each other

toxicity How harmful or poisonous something is

trailblazing Introducing new ideas or methods

trilogy A group of three books or movies

trophy hunter Someone who hunts big game animals such as rhinos and bears for recreation

Vietnam War A war (1955–1975) between China and U.S.S.R.-supported North Vietnam and U.S.-backed South Vietnam

World War II A war (1939–1945) in which the Axis Powers (Germany, Italy and Japan) were defeated by an alliance that included Great Britain, Canada, the United States, and the Soviet Union

zoology The scientific study of animals

FOR MORE INFORMATION

BOOKS

Heitkamp, Kristina Lyn. *Rachel Carson: Pioneering Environmental Activist* (Spotlight on Civic Courage: Heroes of Conscience). New York, NY: Rosen Young Adult, 2018.

Rowell, Rebecca. *Rachel Carson Sparks the Environmental Movement* (Great Moments in Science). Minneapolis, MN: Core Library, 2016.

Stefoff, Rebecca. *The Environmental Movement: Then and Now* (America: 50 Years of Change). North Mankato, MN: Capstone Press, 2018.

Wood, Alix. *Rachel Carson* (World-Changing Scientists). New York, NY: PowerKids Press, 2019.

WEBSITES

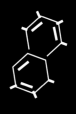

Biography—www.famousscientists.org/rachel-carson
An account of Carson's life and her scientific work.

Quotations—https://bit.ly/3eumrbG
A collection of quotations by Carson about the environment and its importance.

Silent Spring—https://bit.ly/2Z2Jt2M
An article about *Silent Spring* and its effects.

Timeline—www.rachelcarson.org/TimelineJS.aspx
A timeline of major events in Carson's life and career.

INDEX